T0062881

Beneath the River

Beneath the River

Lisy Kuriakose

PARTRIDGE

To order additional copies of this book, contact
Toll Free 800 101 2657 (Singapore)
Toll Free 1 800 81 7340 (Malaysia)
orders.singapore@partridgepublishing.com

www.partridgepublishing.com/singapore

LISY KURIAKOSE HAILS FROM KERALA, SOUTHERN STATE OF INDIA, PRESENTLY WORKING IN KUWAIT. LISY IS A WELL KNOWN WRITER, SOCIAL AND CULTURAL ACTIVIST IN KUWAIT. SHE IS A POST GRADUATE AND GOOD ORATOR TOO. WRITING IS HER PASSION FROM CHILD HOOD. HER FIELD OF INTEREST ARE POEMS, SHORT STORIES AND DRAMS.

SHE HAS PUBLISHED 4 BOOKS

AN ANGEL'S SILENCE (POEMS)

VANITHA PRESIDENT (DRAMAS)

MALAKAHAMAARUM BHUMIYILE CHIRSMASUM (SHORT STORIES)

IDAVAPPATHIYILE PUUMARAM (POEMS)

SHE HAS A VERY SUPPORTIVE FAMILY, HUSBAND THOMAS KURIAKOSE, CHILDREN - LINCY, LEJOE AND GRAND CHILDREN

ADDRESS: ELAVINAMANNIL HOUSE, OMALLOOR, PATHANAMTHITTA, KERALA, INDIA

EMAIL: LISY.KURIAKOSE@GMAIL.COM

Preface

Poet Lisy has taken topics, matters, concept and ideas from life and nature, common to each one but woven a magic around them with words, verse, rhymes and feelings. If anything pleases our mind due to it's perfect blend in design, colour combination, lighting, structure and that perfection is poetry.

Lisy has succeeded in providing to all age group as a sculptor silently carving his fully developed sculpture mentioned in the title poem " Beneath the River". The present Hi Tech. swipe generation and internet whiz kids hardly know what poets and poetry do to our society and their contribution towards humanities. In fact words are magic which can heal, generate life and console all distressed minds. The contribution of Lisy is highly appreciable, as she exalted the status of Indian community in Kuwait, by writing this book in the dominant language of the world, hence accessible to all people and proved that language is not a barrier.

The 51 poems in this book touch many instances in our daily life, or we see diversified lives, unnoticed by common people. The merit of a poet lies when he/she picks up subjects from life. The first poem "The Inheritor is a best example of black comedy. Other poems –Turtles' Life, A Chef , Unseen sobbings will really melt the hearts of the readers. A Twilight, Four winds, First Flower of the Spring and Mother Nature show a poet's passion in mingling with nature. She also expresses her concern over shortness of life and the struggles of soul after death. Going through the poems, we can see the transformation of the poet as Philosopher, Mother, Preacher, Spiritual Leader, Benevolent person and Guide.

This book is really an asset with its content and matters.

Indexes

Poem 1

Inheritor

A movement inside the tomb,
Marked the arrival of a new dead body,
The old, decayed body felt irritant:
And said "I am the owner of this tomb,
Are you encroaching my space?

"Other than few bones and scattered hairs.
What else in your relics?
Then, what for more spaces?"
The new one uttered sarcastically.

After a while it continued…….
"Look at my silvery shining robe;
Besides the costly spices anointed on me
Whose fragrance surpasses even the profound perfumes"

Now they reached to the brim of a war
Seeing their hostile nature,
From the corner of the tomb,
The wriggling worms -
giggled and winked.

"Why? you argue more,
Seek an amicable solution"

Astounding to their surmise,
A sound, from a great distance:
Penetrating the firmament of the sky,
Echoed on the walls of the tomb.

'You, silly, end the dispute and chaos
Ask WORLD BANK who is the real inheritor"

Poem 2

A Search For Thee

In the wonder delight, I search for Thee,
And my chances are too grim.
Still I boasted, I will find Thee
When and where, I don't discern.

I look at the trekking cloud,
Which moves like cotton roll,
My mind is wavery, feet are slippery,
Rhythm of beats are rapid.

Do I lost my sense, where am I?
My queries remain unanswered.
Wild thrush held its beak high,
Pondering relief upon me.

Mild breeze lulled me gently,
As if to share my grievances.
Oh! Thee You are lovey-dovey,
Being a knick-knack on my forehead.

I searched for Thee every nook and corner,
A whistling sound echoed apart,
Upholding a distinctive message,
"Lend your ears towards me"

A drizzling figure appeared there,
Soon it enlightened more vivid,
Whispered to me "to deny self"
Otherwise Thee would be unattainable.

"Painful, too painful" I crunched,
Too difficult to deny self,
And bewildered to the brim of insanity,
What to adopt to forsake?

Meantime memories flashed in me,
Reminding my in vain search with self,
Ha, I unbridled the uncouth self,
To brood Thee in me for ever.

Poem 3

Unseen Sobbings

Looking so tired,
Merging the whole world's pity,
Poor cattle are hobbling aimless,
Being ignorant about the travel to the silent world.

No kingdom, no protection,
Dumb and unaware about their in vain birth,
No vigour, but pain shadowed in the eyes,
Seeking kindness?
Do we care? Of course not:
Why? They are for austerity.

Among them who is slightly healthy,
Diverted from the line for a greenish tip,
Suddenly, a long stick is whirled in the air,
Ha! A loud flash on the back.

Tear drops, reflect a river of sorrows,
Waging tails, fighting against whistling flies,
Dragging the hooves, a step forward,
Where? to escape from butcher's knife.

No, absolutely not, but to become a prey,
So painful, and moments of agony pass,
Repeat this process from auld lang syne,
To be appeared in the form of delicious dishes.

We enjoy in the calm and musical delight,
Demand more for stomach full,
No gratitude, no pricking conscious,
Hoity-toity prances and over rules,
Dumb cries vanish behind the curtains.

Poem 4

A Twilight

The hills near the grey down valley are visible,
As the chariot of the moon appeared in the horizon,
Sun begins to rest after the day's tiresome toil,
The crown of stars hang over us glimmered.
The clouds mounted, backup everything,
Projecting and rising each moment.
On the blue sky, the red holes, seem –
Like a red carpet woven over it.

My eyes roamed over the hidden controls of lights,
The breeze hummed, faint, rather a rhymed hum,
Like the beehives heard at a great distance.
Countless beams gleamed a reddish tone,
Patches of red, sky's cheek flushed with excitement.
As a gambler makes a fast shuffle,
A sudden change on the face of the sky,
Earth has nothing to do, but gazed with amazement,

A touching sight at the sky,
The beauty of the twilight:
A silent delight,
Peace, so deep, in its splendor bright,
Islands, seas, breezes and billows –
All are gathered in the spectacular show,
The red bleeps, magnificent to human eyes,
Branch from sun, glow and diminish.

A passion, quite odd; unveiled gradually,
A morbid fascination of the artistic talents behind,
Shapes, colours, so mystical are flourished on the sky,
How elegant! A ballet dance on a peculiar stage,
Twilight, twilight, a marvelous sight.

Poem 5

Beneath The River

A sculptor strolled on the face of the earth,
Longed to carve a unique art,
Crossed all the hills and valleys,
To find an idol for his art.

There a sculpture stood on the bank,
Engraved on a reddish precious stone,
A stone neither ruby nor its variety,
No one could value the real worth.

The whittler swayed across the bank,
Astonished over the splendid art,
A unique piece, unique among all,
Who had carved this real figure?

The moment he regained his sense,
Gazed the encircling valley behind,
Thousands of half carved statues there;
And were thrown in the cradle of wonder.

Kindled the curiosity in his mind,
Would there be an impetus behind?
A valley of statues all imperfect,
Except the one of worthwhile art,

How did this sculpture appear there?
A myth, a strange myth revolving it,
Vanquished all the so called myths,
Melting all hearts, even stony hearts.

A heavenly maiden, so elegant,
Set a jaunt around the universe,
Flew hither and thither with a thrilling heart,
And wondered over the magnificent earth.

No permission was granted to her,
In any way to mingle with human beings,
The moment such thing would happen,
Nothing, but a sculpture for ever.

Blinked the glimpse of a brook,
Clad in silver garment, flowing-
Crystal clear, while infants played,
Rainbows in sprinkled water.

Her mind fluttered over the innocence,
Wished to spare few moments there,
Flew down and down to be with them,
For an afresh and unceasing memory.

Adopted the form: a pretty child,
Joined with the children there,
Paddled and swam to and fro,
What a splendid moment! She sighed.

Strange feelings strangled on her body,
A kind of fear crawled in mind,
Skipped and tramped on the bank,
In the flicker of eye lid-
Attained original figure.

She pitied on her limits
No wonder, feet stranded there,
A marvelous and glittering piece,
Glancing towards the horizon too yonder.

Lamented over the veiled destiny,
Pleaded for mercy to her master,
Rejected her plea at the first stage, then
Granted pardon on one condition.

"Any day a sculpture would carve,
A sculpture personify you in true spirit,
Even shape and colour exactly similar,
That moment you would regain the original form".

Spread the story crossing the horizon,
Many whittlers rich and poor in fame,
In group or pair even lonely strove,
With no count of days, months and years.

Brought all kinds of precious stones,
In vain their efforts, no match to the red,
The smashing, brilliant and glimmering red,
Endured as a challenge for all sculptors.

No changes by seasons passed,
Still she sobbed on her indefinite fate,
Repented over the childish mind,
And awaited for a savior, a true whittler.

Perceived on the mystery behind,
He contemplated in mind, a moment,
Why I should not attempt a bit?
Before carving my unique figure.

Many mocked at him over his lunatic idea,
Could he triumph, where renowned failed,
Can an earthwork hold its head
Like a cobra who holds its hood?

Procured a piece of reddish rock,
Futile to others, for him worthy,
Started to carve on day and night,
With valiant nature, but no rest.

Drenched in rain, wet in dew,
Keeping hunger and thirst apart,
With no notice of sunset and rise,
Like a soldier who fights till last.

The barren rock slowly turned,
A dexterity of dedicated work,
A personification of real beauty,
A sculpture exactly similar to that.

Bloomed the eyelids like a rose,
With wonder and delight united,
Jumped up with exceeding joy,
A satisfaction after unfeigned toil.

Still no change in the old sculpture,
Although he carved the same one,
Yet, the red, dazzling red,
Remained as a question in front.

Deplored over the impeccability,
Panic in mind, punched the statue,
But, it bruised his finger a bit,
And blood oozed through it.

A drop, a tiny drop, fell on the statue,
Sudden a brilliance spread on the spot,
Reddish same as the brilliant red-
A rival complexion of the peculiar art.

Deepened the bruise as fast as he could,
Glutted the blood over the sculpture,
He became doughy and blemished:
but delighted,
While the brilliance was diffused over it.

Fainted and fell down
On the feet of the figure,
Feckless and motion almost seized,
A fluttering noise echoed there, while,
The sculpture wanted to move a step.…..

A gleam entered in his inflexible eyelids,
And his pale eyes blotted the maiden,
"The unique one longed so far,
At last I carved: he murmured.

Poem 6

New Way

Rhythm of life lost any where,
Now wake up for a new dawn,
The ebb and flow always unleash us
Changing rhythms change the world too.

Let the political races bombard with bad news,
Along with dull and murky future of economy,
Keep the cold, darker days in oblivion,
So a new shoot will sprout out for all.

Wake up for the impending gift of a new beginning.
Wake up to walk on the straight path,
Wake up from our dogmatic slumbers,
As the new light of life not at par.

Life is packed with significant events
Though every one of us comes up against -
the rough side of life,
It is all about resolutions and reinventions,
And we have to do a lot always.

No need to be loomed in frustration,
Or grope in darkness as a blind does,
A new way to be opened to sustain,
The universe and its creatures.

Poem 7

Success

I am not a success in the eyes of the world
I don't have a big mansion,
I don't hold great position,
Nor being any award winner,
Nor my books sold in many numbers,
Or appeared my photo in magazine cover,
In spite of these, still I feel a success.

When my child hug me with love,
When my pet looks me with adoring eyes.
When I share a laugh with a poor worker,
When I extend a hand to the needy,
When my simple words touch the heart of any-
I feel it as a success

Amid the mishaps,
I count the blessings of God,
The regularity of the seasons,
The reliability and rhythm of nature
The unfading glory of the stars,
The tremendous healing power of time
And the ever sustaining power of hope;
The bountiful hearts yearning for love
And the non perishing souls hunger for prayer;
The endless and diligent quest for truth
And the deepest struggle for justice
The non stopping urge to create,
And the valiant will to overcome.

Always count these on the array of success,
Apart from things to hold us on this uncertain world.

Poem 8

Mission

Every one has a mission to accomplish
To be in line with our vision or not,
To distinguish the real mission,
Certainly, a great task.
Oh! we born and live for many causes,
For war or peace, who judges last?
Life itself is a war,
For some, chances of peace are remote
And eventually, seek shade under the bitter gourd
Never think, a worm or dry wind can wither it.

Poem 9

A Wedding At Cana

Lovely wedding, charm and merry,
Decorated the antechamber,
A lavish feast,
To thrill and enthrall the guests.

Among them, Jesus, His disciples –
And Mother Mary too,
An unforeseen situation,
A wear and tear on certain faces,
Wine, not a drop,
Even for a sip…
Mother of Jesus intervened,
And wished to ease the entangled situation.

The precautious mind in her,
In the midst of trouble to be calm,
Had an insight about son's ability.
Something she conveyed to the servants,
"Do as He directs:
At first Jesus was not hasty,
As His fullness of time had not yet come.
The situation, catalyzed the obedient servants,
Who all wished to see a miracle as Mary's clue.

There were many valuable cauldrons,
To be used in an auspicious occasion,
Jesus did notice none of them,
Other than the earthen wares kept out,
Used for cleaning the feet.
And He ordered the servants to fill,
By drawing water from the well.

They filled up to the brim,
Without a break in time.

An enchanting sound pierced the water,
The sound of the Great creator!
A sound similar to that of creation time:
Now a shiver and shudder on water,
As if a change occurred in matter,
No where to hide,
Neither to the side,
Nor to the bottom,
Strangled to spill and run,
But, tightly packed not to turn,
Smirked to conceal the fear,
Smirked again in tear,
Eventually –
Peace and glory paired,
A brownish tan appeared,
An entire transformation:
Sparkling, golden wine's so swift calibration.

Here, collapsed the wheel of history,
To replace with the talents mastery.

Tasted the delicious wine all the males,
As a rare quality from a rare sale,
Ha! Wine, intoxicating so deep,
They commented while they sipped.

Now the chariot of modern history rolls,
A history with JESUS in center,
Now, a similar wedding is imperative,
For a great transformation,
And transfiguration too,
A cup of holy wine to sip,
To be intoxicated by the Holy Spirit,
To replenish and revive God's kingdom,
To get rid of man's boredom.

Poem 10

Turtles' Life

Lazy, but gay, I was lying,
Some where on the white sand,
Gazing over the horizon,
Or looking at the calm sea.

Hardly any waves there,
Instead ripples were dancing in the wind,
The sand was swirled in a corner.
I could not believe my eyes,
Thousands of hatched baby turtles,
Wading the sand, towards the sea.

A search for the mother,
A wish to be lulled by tender touch,
Mother,
Mother,
Either a riddle or an imagination,
No one here to solve it.

Sill they were lingering and paddling,
Distance to cover very little,
But,
A struggle for existence:
Life....
Life is a hunt,
For each and every one,
The foundation is unjust,
And grievances are the corner stones.

Thousands of seagulls were circling above,
Competing to have this delicious prey,
A battle for life and a battle for prey,
An unceasing battle on the face of the earth.

Many wriggled in their sharpened claws,
Survived ones paddled to the shore,
The frivolity of waves drifted them
back to the coast,
As pushing the defeated soldiers –
again the battle front.

Poor turtles were again the victims of gulls,
Only a few who won the battle of life,
Reached the depth of the sea safely,
To continue their exploration –
for a mother and life.

Poem 11

Prayer

Prayer is a silent whisper,
Conscious or subconscious mind reflects,
Filling goodness and overflowing joy,
No barriers, fortress or distances,
Nothing stops this mighty weapon.
It is potent, vigorous and tranquil too,
Besides, expels enormous strength and spirit,
It is uniting all and ignoring parity.
The millions utter praises always,
Emit magnanimity, love and sacrifice
in high measure.
A weapon for the feeble and mighty as well,
A medicine for wretched hearts,
A cleanser for the sinner sighing deep,
A divine path for all cast and creed,
A guiding star in murky life,
An anchor or beacon in a roaring sea.

It echoes in the wilderness, mountains, valleys and bushes,
Desert may flourish, barren land may fertile,
Empire may crumble in its mightiness,
A unique medium of overwhelming joy,
Soothing, reviving and glorifying all.

It can travel crossing the oceans
And firmament of sky,
And has no deviation
Till it reaches the destination.

Poem 12

Would There Be Sin

Bright sunny morning singing birds,
Could not soothe her curious mind,
Eve wished to be obstinate,
To quench her inquisitive mind.

The mere countenance of the
Magnificent creature,
Changed her more delightful.
Chatted each other superseding old comrades
All her detest and conceit were melted
Although she fancied nervous.

Adding surprise to her surmise –
it turned as a trustworthy pal.
Eve, in the meantime,
Reached a stage of pliancy,
Under the magic spell of artificial -
induced ecstasy.

The slumbering passions woke up in her
"No, no" she murmured,
Not to consult Adam,
No, nothing can be forbidden,
I want dominion of all
My right, my pleasure to eat the forbidden fruit,
I can solace myself with its special effects"

"Oh! Adam have this succulent fruit,
Never you tasted the same before,
Sure it would be more sweeter than
My sweet heart"
Thousands of commands were in her deep blue eyes,
To Adam her charming words –
were seemed as sweet hymn,
Helpless could not resist her free will,
He proved himself so common as any other man,
Forgot his Master and His commands,
Paved the way for the first step of sin,
If Adam resisted, would there be sin?

Poem 13

Voyage

A voyage for a longer distance,
This is the aim of each person,
Like a voyage in ocean liner,
Which anchors in the depth not on shallow.

Why does the voyage not a success?
It is not a dream, but a stream:
In the beginning small ripples lull,
As goes further mountains and hills to cross.

Open the window at day time,
Get the light required for a longer voyage,
Let an iron door shut the yesterday,
Not to brood again as it is dead.

Never dream for the unborn tomorrow,
It may be born or half way die,
Bread of today is easy to munch,
Bread of yesterday perhaps fetid.

Bread of tomorrow is not even baked,
Keep the anxiety and wear apart,
Plan constructively as best as you can
Never keep on the brink of two boats.

Good thinking leads to logical causes,
And bad thinking to worry and tension,
Welled up tears are no more a remedy,
Impair your mental strain, so do one task at time.

There are appalling scenes in life,
When we stand in midst of life,
While we accumulate the dead yesterdays
The present flies its own way.

We are in the meeting place of two eternities,
The vast past, which endured for ever,
The future that plunges on the last syllable,
In the middle a short present to live.

Live sweetly, lovely and purely,
Before the sun fades for a nap,
Lift yourself from the despondency,
And pave the way for courage to come in.

Every day is new as a tender flower
Have the fragrance before it fades and falls
We only can make or mar our destiny.
Be vibrant and careful on the voyage.

Poem 14

A Cobbler

Before the dawn his poignancy,
Pushes him to the streets,
Squatting near a wall or under a lamp post,
Opens the bundle with a shivering hand,
He gibbers aloud with a broken heart,
Do you need a cobbler to mend your shoes?

Most remain impassive,
Or pay a deaf attention,
Feeling shy and proud about their status,
Nobody views on his pitiful life,
Or never plaudit on his sincere work.

Some cast a look fills with odium,
As if they get detracted by his presence,
And think even he desecrates the society,
Which is symbol of their prestigious life.

To high society he is a worm,
But to his family he is a gleam.

During the work he perplexes,
About the replete poverty at his shack,
His ambition is for a half stomach mean,
As a piquant meal is only a dream.

In the streets his sound echoes,
On the petrified heart of the society.

Poem 15

Lamentations Of Earth

I lament over my children's deeds,
My chuckle is vanished,
And sobbing lash on the horizon,
My dreams are lost,
Where cupids and fairies are dancing,
Fear of fret is near,
As I sob cheerlessly,
Glistening streams run trickling,
Down my cheeks, I keep aside all,
And lament over the pitiful days ahead.

I carry a heavy load for you,
No one notice my pathetic stress,
You are always on the way to cheat,
Cheat and loot your own brother.
I store and spread all my treasures
Only for you, still..?

Diminishing treasures,
Disordering genetic factors,
May change my rhythm as a whole,
As years drop, for coming generation,
Eventually I turn as a fairy tale.
You are too nice in your semblance,
While I master to keep the balance.

You pull out my hairs so mercilessly,
Which serve as green cladding on me,
You tear out my silver brocades too,
Keeping me nude…
My chest is warm, warmer than ever,
A small prick on it may turn worse,
Do I take some precautions for all?

Oh! Children your atrocities are more,
Snowballing the sectarian violences,
And blood flows like a brook,
Making me to glow red hot.
The repercussion of my lamentations,
Provoke me to loose my control very often,
Then I spew in the form of a volcano,

Some times I shed my tears,
Which is an out break of my sorrows,
For you may be a heavy flood or tsunami,
What else left to sooth myself?
In both cases I loose some of my children,
But I bear, just for the sake of the other,
My patience is undermining,
For rejuvenating your motto,
How long? The question in my front,
And keeping ceaseless this trend..

Poem 16

Vineyard

In my dream I plant a vineyard,
Near the brook to be ever green,
I toil for the fullness of beauty,
It looks like a crown of glory.

I guard it day and night,
Fight against thorns and briers,
I wait for the vineyard –
To blossom and put forth shoots.

One day its branches reach the high heaven,
The boughs bend and fill with fruits,
To shine as the head of a rich valley,
And a shelter for many creatures.

Oh! Eastern Wind, be mild and gentle
Don't drive the tender flowers like chaff,
Neither let the leaves to wither,
Nor drop the raw fruits to be trodden under feet.

Instead allow it to yield in its season,
Let all the fruits reel with vine,
To proclaim the wondrous deeds of God,
Even for the generations to come.

Poem 17

Dreams

Wonderful dreams are fairy queens,
Soothing, comforting and charming,
Sweet, sudden, lengthy and cruel too,
Certain times, a reflection of bitter reality.

How nice, you pay silent visit in sleep,
Accompany with pleasures of heaven,
Where your origin is?
A land beyond our imagination?

How you perform thousand of miracles,
By changing every one as kings, queens,
Or any one as you wish,
Enabling to mediate on your unusual skills,
By ignoring their precious times.

Many weave new dreams always,
And try to fulfill their desires in life,
To gain a sort of satisfaction,
At least for a moment as wished.

Your world of pleasures are confined to us,
The illusions are marvelous and splendid,
We try to speculate and analyze you,
In vain, cannot master you any time.

Poem 18

Four Winds

Oh! Four winds of the world, mighty spirits,
Like a multicolor ribbon you hang on earth,
Black – Western, maker of thunder and rain,
Pretty – holy white, keeper of north,
Rejuvenator and cleanser of the world,
Alluring and energetic Red – Pillar of East
You sparkle light and shoot up the morning stars,
And distribute wisdom to men, for conquering life.
Meek and magnificent yellow- master of south,
If you close the eyes, no seasons and no mankind,
Power of growth remain still and infertile.

Oh! Four spirits, you are united in one knot,
Which cannot be broken or released.
Father sky – the highest of all,
Spreads his arms wide,
Glances the merits and demerits,
And wishes men's thoughts,
Always be the highest,
As eagles fly up and up.

Mother earth – another word of patience,
Clad in white and buckskin dress,
Considers all living beings as her children,
Allowing to suck her overflowing love.

Will a holy tree flourish in our hearts
For a vision mighty and true?
To get rid darkness from eyes before lost,
To make ourselves an offering for all,
And to leave visible tracks to follow.

Poem 19

A Weary Traveller Of Night

Lost my way, I tramped in dark,
As I crossed the dense forest,
The dusk grew old,
I was more terrified,
Of the shaping gloom inside,
And the unlit night in its perfection.

Lonely on my way, hardly any companion,
No crickets, no nightingale,
Neither a cacophony nor a tweet,
So mystic and congenial,
And moments passed age long.
"A wandering mind has nothing to do,
Other than chanting prayers for all".

In the dense thickets,
I saw two burning eyes,
Whose gleam penetrated around.
My blood turned so icy,
A shiver from toe to head,
And my gloom was about to burst.

Suddenly I struck a lonely figure,
Wounded and fatigued,
Like a warrior fought in the battle,
Till his efforts turned futile.
Yet, the burning gleam,
Resembled the moonlights-
Pierced through the tree tops.

A sudden creak, that too feeble,
Broke the silence of night,
In my front an aged lioness –
Pretty pride in her glorious past,
Now looked like a hag.

I struck the bell of past,
Alas, no clues in any part,
My blood warmed slightly, sprouting,
An acquaintance figured with compassion.

Her eyes too budded;
An emphatic exclamation.

Poem 20

Sobbings Of Time

Time flies as birds fly,
But, invisible to human eyes,
The flaps of its wing –
echoes too far.
All colours are bright and beautiful,
Red, green and white –
Are resembling the time.
Red reflects yesterdays,
Green for today,
And white for tomorrow.

The stains of yesterday,
Shadowed on the face of white,
Too difficult to be cleaned,
As sobbing of many creations,
Deeply rooted there.
To catch these expression-
is a miserable plight,
Which at length ends void.
The vacuum occurred,
Were the wounds on yesterday's chest,
The embodiment,
The strength,
The flow, all frosted.

But, today, a slight melting,
Salt in the tears,
Pains in deep sighs,
Useless the efforts,
To link the broken nerves,
As the cracks are so deep.

Many arose before,
To link the generations,
Where days were dead,
Evenings were with frost,
Silence nested and,
nightmares perched.

In the corridor of time,
Even now, a sound,
The sound of thousands of martyrs,
Sobbing and lashing on the walls.

Poem 21

Phase of life

How many phases life has?
Three phases,
First one void and null,
Utter stillness slumbers,
On the footstep of centuries,
As frivolity lost in the long run.

All winds were fastened,
So no motion at all,
No fret, everything was stationery,
Even the souls were in oblivion,
Here is the beginning,
Where the door of Hades opens.

Second phase, full of motion,
Which overwhelms the motionless past,
While embracing,
A spirit wave is inducing,
The boiling bubbles in the pitcher of time,
This alludes and entails the present era.
Simmering feelings stretch to heights,
Brooding sparrows are chirping,
Wings folded moths sucking nectar,
A trifling amusement!.

Chain of the second phase lead,
Where,
Fame had fallen short of truth,
The affability and condescension,
Are enough to reckon the spiritless past.

The third phase,
The truth, untold truth dies,
On
Terrible faces and smiling faces,
With no notice of survival,
Centuries may be many ahead,
Similar to that hid behind the curtains.
Again motion ceases, past echoes,
Keeping the present still moving,
To stir an oscillation to and fro,
It can be bitter or better,
But the earth is gloomy in this threat.

Poem 22

A Chef

No one notices what a chef does,
Most chefs tend to be introverts and shy,
Whether they are celebrity chefs or acclaimed one.
They stay in the background than be in-
Center stage with spotlight shining on them.

Joy is rippling on their face seeing-
others enjoy their food,
And more than once eating in his
restaurant.

They are standing in the shadows near the kitchen,
Watching people with delight in his culinary creations,
And beaming in happiness at seeing the diners' enjoyment.

Most will never shake hands with them,
Never bother to seek him out to say "Thank You",
Or send letter of appreciation to his restaurant,
A near time or at some later points,
Never does the chef strolls through the dining room,
Tacitly and subtly soliciting praises,
They are mostly contented to look upon people's -
delights afar.

Poem 23

Christmas Too Yonder

Christmas at hand, a Christmas Eve,
A merry and merry one....
Merry for whom?
Many make it merry for themselves, but,
Many can't afford it make it merry.

It may cost enough to keep merry,
The frail spark of luxury,
Is a ridiculous fashion,
The hail pours to every rift and key hole,
Has ceased to vibrate,
The last stroke of twelve.

My sense floated in the air,
Linking with thousands of thoughts of the past,
The joy I ever had, the bitter spots in life

A lonely boy, abandoned and forsaken,
Cold, bleak and biting weather,
The rain, the hail and the sleet,
Doomed to wander through the world,
The dead silence of the night,
An atmosphere where life is altered.

Deep black garment of the night-
A dark robe of darkness,
Conceals the sins of the world,
As the night cannot detach the darkness,
And same for man to give up his sins,
Or the vague uncertain happiness thrilling,
An inner call comes out of every one,
"lead, lead to the right path".

The shudder of the earth,
The heavenly sky,
The mysterious appearance-
of the unique star,
The rhythm of trumpet of the angels,
Songs of the nightingales,
An invitation to the joyful world.

Piercing the eagerness,
A new borne's cry, beside the straw,
Where, the breeze pretty stiff to lull,
The God of Past, Present and Future,
The tenderness of love,
Full of promises and encouragement.
The world sleeps in His smile,
In His pleasure of thoughtfulness,
Tranquility restores, perplexity eases.

Now, cheer with the Christmas,
The churchyards and homes,
With glistening dews on the top,
Burning lanterns high and bright,
Along with the blaze of milky light,
Strangles with dingy mist,
Descended from mountain's chest.

Yet, we are rattling emptiness of heart,
By pulling selfish fashions cart,
Burn the fragrance of love,
Rather than the incense of richest shrines,
Otherwise –
A merry Christmas with earnest in heart
will be too yonder.

Poem 24

Flower And The Butterfly

How lovely you pretty flower!
Which artist engraved you miraculously?

The errant butterfly mumbled to the flower,
To outwit it in a flicker.

The panegyric pleased the flower too much
And lifted to the ether of the sky,
It enthralled and dribbled the nectar,
Never knowing the swindle behind.

Oh! My dear, your murmur seems-
A marvelous euphony,
Rivals the great musician of the world,
Come and enshrine in my heart.

The haughty flower splashed and envious look,
To others who were glimmered and shrieked,
Without thinking of its' fate.

As evening shadow fell on the plant,
It longed restlessly for the dawn,
To share the agony of the night,
With the butterfly at any cost.

At dawn, the errant butterfly glided away,
Neither cast a soggy look,
Or remembered its tender promises,
Instead, hovered over another with full nectar.

The flower gibbered on its mutation,
As its grandeur had been spilled,
And honey dwindled.
It lamented over its frailty and pride
And accepted life as an enigma.

Poem 25

Me and you

Are we the two sides of the coin?
Either you may be the number,
Or I am the logo,
Me and you vary in everything,
Although made up of same stuff.

You stimulate the rhythm of universe,
And trumpet in every corners.
My face is full of spots and specks,
A reflection of the pain of life,
Nothing is available to sooth me,
And all pleasures are under your feet.
Who makes these parities?

Lisy Kuriakose

Now,
In your laugh my joy overwhelming,
In your eyes, my sorrows overflow,
I traveled afar without you,
But I lost myself.

In the darkness, you whispered to someone,
All about my goodness, which I never noticed.
Your consolation seemed a great revelation to me,
You are an Oak tree!
And me, simple grass….
Even then, you said, still say,
We are the two sides of the same coin.

Poem 26

Ladies

Ladies in the new millennium,
Still their life a farce drama,
No one notices their pathetic cry,
All are lashing on the petrified hearts--
No motion, no empathy at all;
As if created for man's pleasure only.
She can stand on her feet,
If she will make the heart stony;
Arrows from all corners of society,
Sure wound her from toe to head,

But, who stands courageously;
The one, who can bear and suffer,
No notice of society's comments.
That only a rich society lady can do;
But poor, common mass,
Representatives of the have not
Still prey for the modern slavery.

Poem 27

Nature

Nature seems to be so precious
Loving and patting me like a mother
I doze in her bosom
How magnificent that feeling itself!
She induces me much
By giving always a tender touch
To bring up my talents mastery
And make a plume in the pages of history.
I worry over greenery lost,
Which was surpassingly envious in the past,
But, how ever man tries to recover the best
Alas! his dreams change her the worst.
Oh mother! I love you always
Throwing my agony behind the ways
I regret over my brothers deeds
Who never recognize the future tides.

Poem 28

An Ode To My Lovely Roses

My days are meaningless, nights sleepless,
Where do I roam, still I roam,
Over shadows and shadows.
Neither a pen, nor a feather or
Ink of any sort to scribble,
But, the blood of my heart
I scribble in its reddish tone.
The pivot of my house: anchor at large,
Now I look corner to corner
I keep my nose for your smell
Waiting eagerly, for winds of earth,
Which bring your smell in their satchel.
News of many type gaze in my mind's corner,
Even stories of your taste too,
And melodies of mesmeric tune,
Where do I open my heart
Burdened with many knots, sizzling, panic
And with pangs of pain,
Yes, I do want to pour;

Poem 29

Liberty

I long for freedom,
Yet, too yonder in the horizon,
Freedom is precious,
Freedom is my right,
Freedom is my whisper –
And the complacency.

A mystic mind's accost is –
Meditating on this great pleasure,
My intrepidity or imagination is too rapid,
Which jumps from admiration to love,

I born as free,
So free, but I cried; why?
The indication mark on my wrist,
First knot of binding,
Symbol of the cords to be bound later

The air is free for me,
Who pollutes it?
As well as the water is free,
But turbid with toxin.

Am in free in thinking?
No, that is also suppressed.
Money, pride and ego exploit –
My freedom always.
These exercise their strength –
And have no eye towards the ill-fated.

I lost my identity,
All are in rage –
To put forth futile plans.
The universe grants equality,
Here, I am curtailed, you are infinite.
Neither in life, nor in death
Alas! No freedom for me.
In life, the rights are denied,
But, observe meaningless rituals-
After the death.

Every one sobs with crocodile tears,
Clad the body with the best dress,
Chant memorial prayers,
The insipidity, the noise,
The self importance in death,
Are no more a solution to their cruelty.
No soul longs for such impertinence,
Every one long for freedom,
That in life, not in death.

Poem 30

A Sonnet Of A Star

The firmament of the sky looks so pretty,
As numerous stars gazed at the antechamber,
Without any anguish in their twinkling eyes,
They are seemed like sporadic gem,
Blinked at the apex,
Or thousands of cedar trees flourished in delight.

Implore to have a tête-à-tête,
And wished to join their hindering meditation,
Their brilliance proclaims the glory of God,
My eyes had soothed at the bounteous sight,
And heart filled with bliss at the innocence.

How celestial and precious are their shooting life!
In the midst of darkness their divine light,
Enlighten the inscrutable ways of passengers,
Giving an inkling against stumbling stones.

Poem 31

Life Divine

What to loose, if life divine,
Bounty is boundless every time,
Deep calls the deep to smile,
Larks sing melodiously all the time.

Valleys blossom as spring comes,
Cataracts seem to be more enchanting,
Aurora is in her best brocade,
Every creature has its own way of happiness.

But man alas! Seems to be pathetic,
Being the crown and glory of God's creation,
Where he loses, when he ignores his mind,
He searches God here and there,
And turns his attempt futile every time.

Poem 32

Death

Come true friend, charming figure,
Never I shudder at your unseen visit,
As if superior to all you claim,
By altering your appearance swiftly.

You are unique in showing parity to all,
Your footsteps are vivid and enchanting,
You enter in glass palaces as well as huts,
Dignity and affluence are nothing to you.

Oh Personification of earnest toil!
From where do acquire intoxication?

For some you are a burning cruel symbol,
Plucking budding and tender life.
You have an embodiment of a lovely bloom,
Which radiates its fragrance all around.

Many lament on your hidden mystery,
You bid emancipation from bondage of flesh,
But, cannot do anything to our immortal souls,
Which is eternal rather than a the decaying flesh.

Poem 33

New Year's Eve

The knell of the old has gone,
The trumpets of the new eve are beating,
This is the time for rejoicing,
Take a new pledge in heart and advance,
And expurgate with meekness of mind.
Retreat for a moment and glance as a whole,
Reckon the loss and gain on the balance of time,
If the loss is more, don't desperate,
Encounter with courage and firmness.
May the failure turn as a success,
Beware in mind if the gain is more,
Don't be proud, humble than ever before,
As an individual or nation it is vital,
To replenish the new strength and vigour,
For accumulating energy to cut the "Gordian knot"
To accomplish the "Herculean task" in front of us,
That to consider the cosmos as one family,
And to bring "Third World' in to first row.

Poem 34

Farewell

To bid farewell seems painful,
But we have to see off any time,
Though, source only unknown:
May be in a nook or corner or in a banquet hall.

Sure, a wistful sorrow hovers here,
The agony melts on the peace ahead,
To fly across the oceans and lands,
To lead a peaceful life in homely land..

To stay a little longer, I hope,
But, who am I on the time of rope,
There I curtail my thoughts a bit,
Where awaits you another destiny bright.

The triumphs we shared in past,
Hope to go on until the last,
Where ever you go, what ever you nurture,
Of course, we keep an unfading picture -
with blissful memories.

Now the pendulum sways to and fro-
Warns the time is near,
Holding tears gush out in pile,
Glitters on cheeks in a placid smile.

Yes we wish you, a fond farewell,
Blotted with love from the last text of heart,
On the streets echoes your valiant footprints,
Good bye as the wheel of time rolls.

Darkness dazzles everywhere,
And perching in the minds too.
See the chaos all around,
Creating dismay and confusion.

There are gleams of hope in the midst
But to identify them and make use,
That is the greatest citadel in front,
Still time, to turn as bright spots again.

Poem 35

Patterns And Shadows Of Life

Yes, I forget to live,
All these years have passed,
Many ups and downs lulled me,
Still I forgot to live,

Passions and great events never touched me,
Mostly I was lonely in my style of life.
No memorable moment to be splashed,
However I unwind the past.

Will a flower ask the plant its welfare
I don't know, why I feel like this
So moody, so gloomy very often
How I could be so cruel
I am a personification of selfishness
Do any one change me like this
Or the bitter some days of life?

My heart is petrifying each moments
The cries of have notes lash feebly now.
Life is full of miseries, no hope, no love,
Meaningless and absurd.

All the chaos, calm and wonder,
Captured in the instant icefall,
The frost draws multi patterns,
On the window pane.

Also paints the leafy splendors,
The bizarre world of frost,
Rich palette of designs,
Alluring sight!.

Minds too draws many designs
All with a melancholic touch
Some where on the outskirts,
Certain times a line of happiness.

While darkness falls on the courtyard,
Hooting and howling the guardians of night,
Wait until darkness overshadows,
A row of angels fluttering their wings
Descending from heaven, say truth is not far.

Poem 36

Father

Never I search you among the dead.
You always live in my heart,
Oh, blissful solitude and guiding light
Be with us till our last breath

Each whisper I feel your presence,
Each sobbing I taste your love,
Each shining star I see your face,
Each moment I cherish your memories.

You never boasted or waited for praises,
Always did your work silently,
You spoke about your dreams very seldom,
And poured your last drop of blood for us.

Poem 37

A Morning After 3000 A.D.

From where do u appear ugly creature?
I heard a rattling sound at a distance.
I was in oblivion and when I could recollect
Enquired feebly,
"Where are my land, seas and forest"?
A reply immediately unfurled there:
"We demolished all your huge buildings and mountains,
Converted everything as plain land,
All of them were messengers' of diseases".

While I awaited for the origin of rattling,
I saw another bright spot-
Sparkling in the corner of horizon,
In the flicker of an eye lid-
It reached to me.

Jumped out of it one murmuring creature,
Which could illuminate the whole surroundings,
It murmured to me,
"Your mere sight is even unbearable to us,
Now we should live in quarantine".
I was in confusion and my eyes roamed,

Looking at my pathetic stage, it continued:
"We know each other, even what one thinks,
But for you it was out of reach.
We have no greed for caste, race and power,
No lust of flesh, pride and vanity,
No more sorrows, poverty and hunger,
By these merits we made you none and nothing"

Poem 38

He

Lost in the horizon for ever,
My thoughts were burned,
In the mighty wind of time,
Paradise loomed beyond the sea,
My hopes were shattered;
Like uprooted trees by a merciless wind.
No way for me, only darkness brooded,
No one to shed a ray of light,
Gloom encircled in my life.

Far, very far,
I saw a man having red hair,
Whom I ignored in my glorious past,
"The man of life and sea of love".
Millions of suns can't excel his brightness,

He called me in calm and passionate voice,
"Come and throw your burdens upon me,
I am mighty enough to sustain you".

All my burdens melted as ice-
In his compassionate voice,
A way, truth and life reopened.

Poem 39

World

How wonder the world itself,
What an immortal hand or power
Who frame this astonishing symmetry?.

The starry, golden spangled sky,
Illuminating bright veined lightning,
Milky moon light and cloud,
Always shower inspiration and enthusiasm,
With glamour and glitter untiring.

Look at the forests, valleys and plains,
Sleeping under the emerald green carpets,
Singing, soaring and alluring,
Canaries, nightingales and colourful birds.

The foam adds a silvery garment,
To the brook which flows smiling,
All these convey a hidden message,
"Life is for toil, not for lethargy,
Each moment is precious and unrecoverable,
Utilize life for fruitful service,
This is the world our creator wants"

Poem 40

Songs Of Spirits

The murmuring sound of morning breeze,
Seemed like a music of victory,
The ebb and flow of the deep wide sea,
Lulled the earth in its laps like a baby.

Here, not beyond from the spots of heaven,
Spirits of dead cheered in tranquility,
As their melancholic past days-
Were in oblivion.

Among them one appeared as lunatic,
Though his sound was perfect and clear,
"I crossed the citadel of earth......",
Screamed loudly, as if he had longed to win.

Now, no barrier between us,
Till yesterday iron hedges prevented us,
I fought until my armour got blood stained,
And dejected on seeing the crumbled empire.
Blindly led by the so-called man.

"Hail, Oh, sing the song of emancipation,
Sing with joy and love for ever."

Poem 41

Figure Of Solitude

Sat on green pastures,
Daughter of perpetual sorrows,
The mild wind scented with rose,
Greased me while I lost in thoughts.

I mourned, if I have wings like dove,
I would fly far and refrain from sorrows,
Twinkling stars smiled on seeing me,
The wild moor feathered its shades,
The moon glanced thorough the gaps of tree trunks,
The ripened corns shone as golden balls,
The melodious music of larks waved there.

Yes, poisonous stings of sorrows hurt a lot,
Amid I could hear the constant whispering of mind,
"A journey places God,
Out of life circle is in vain always,
Replace Him in center and move accordingly.

Poem 42

A Writer

A writer always gropes where he can,
To pick out substance for his scribbling,
In a market, in a slum, in a castle,
Where his characters dwell.

His mind is always restless and wavers,
Till the character plays the real role,
He cries, laughs and expresses emotions,
Each time they leave transitional period.

He writes for society, seldom for his sake,
Uses his pen against the injustice in society.

A wandering mind has no notion,
In the notch and front it varies,
Often thinks of performing great,
Suddenly everything lashes on the floor.

Selfish people all round, none can perform great,
Things are assessed on the moment's action,
No criteria has set behind to measure the truth,
Who is the master amidst of lot of fixes.

Poem 43

Again The Bud Blooms

I am thrilled to bloom as a colourful flower,
Thousands of butterflies hover over me,
Even the breeze lulls and pats me,
To dribble my fragrance at once upon blooming.

I never realize in them,
My beloved, a personification of love,
I am fully immersed in dream,
And awaiting my idol of love to come near.

"One day my beloved with words of nectar,
Tickle me till I reach a blissful state,
And in that divine touch,
My meaningless birth become enriched."

While I was swimming in that sweet memories,
They came, hiding their treachery, disguised as friends,
Not listening my sobbing nor bothering my pain,
Squeezed and sipped my life, punched my soft body.

After shooting out their scornful arrows
They ran away from my miserable state,
Petals fallen, axis broken,
Fell on the ground for passers to tramp
Still, my soul's energy glows so holy.

Being graceful, never my birth become futile,
Until the last ray of hope remains in me,
Here my vision my fruitful anticipation
To continue for many generations.

I have nothing more to perform
To accomplish the unquenched lusts
Other than rebirthing as a fresh and stunning bud,
Until my beloved one reaches.

Poem 44

The Flourished Tree In Monsoon

A flourished tree
Under the umbrella of sky,
With flowers from trunk to base,
Gorgeously reigning time,
One day, a tiny water drop requested,
"Will you be kind enough:
To grant a little space inside your flowers
To hide and protect my body from the scorching sun"

The flourished tree retorted
Oh! my flowers are filled with nectar and fragrance
And if I give you space, it will turn also displeasing -
with your impurity.

Gloomy and lost, with no way in front,
The water drop accepted the cruelty of the burning rays,
Joined with it many other drops too
Who did not get space on earth,
Reached to the heights of the sky;
And spread a black blanket
To pave the way for the monsoon.
As the wind lashed mercilessly
The drops turned as a down pour.

The delighted pitter patter rain drops,
Tickled the flowers to steal their treasures,
Before flowing down like a brook.

The butterflies longed to have nectar,
Hovered down on the flowers,
Found their petals fully sodden,
And no nectar to dribble out,
Commented sarcastically, then hovered to the heights.

A sudden shiver and shock-
Crept over the sodden flowers,
They pitied and lamented bitterly
As their nectar flown down and fragrance lost.

Looking at their pathetic condition,
The parent tree pleaded to the rain,
"So tender and lovely are my offspring,
Who should be embraced so gently,
And not by your pitter patter hard blows"

The rain drops blew the trumpet of victory.
And responded in a sardonic way,
"Is it possible to embrace your lovely tiny tots,
With our hands which are so unclean?"

As no way left out, the proud tree pledged
"I will never bloom until the monsoon over"

Poem 45

Mind

Mind
A riddle.
A riddle which can never be solved,
by uncoiling the traps,
it would be more rigid.

Mind
An ocean of love
Even the whirlpools fill,
There are ripples of love menacing.

Mind
A glass vessel
If it falls to the ground
It shatters into thousands of pieces
And cannot be fixed in the original shape

Mind
A magic horse,
A horse that cannot be harnessed,
With bit and bridle.
Though it crosses fields, forests and valleys
And grazes on the peaks..

Mind

A magic mirror,
A mirror which reflects many colours and lines.
Line extends to infinity,
Colour blends another colour;
And finally whiteness appears.

Mind

A magic box
A box which has many lids and cavities,
Filled with secret mysteries,
Along with smells of ancient time,
Which forces out to go as lid lifts.

Mind

A volcano
Always belches out emotions,
Varies from meekness to cruelty,
Most time in a dormant stage,
But, it has moments of peace
As well as moments of explosion.

Mind

An oasis
By its fantasy nature
It creates a greenery
And as we approach it moves far and far.

Mind

Perhaps a breeze, a tempest or a cyclone
No one knows
When a wind blows or its origin
Similar the existence and -
Appearance of mind is unknown

Poem 46

Wind And Butterfly In Search Of Genes

Flowers, everywhere flowers
A sea of beauty, a cosmos of brilliance,
Sizes and shapes vary,
Even the typical style reflects
The freshness, newness,
Eyes get blinked in their radiant beauties,
But,
The breeze expresses it's unlikeness,
"Hey, I cross all these distances,
The mountains and valleys, burrows and all
Only to have your perfumes,
Yes, my life springs up in your scents,
Now, what do I fill in my satchel,
Pretty petals in vibrant colours?
I agree, shapes even matchless, yet no use,
From time immemorial you enrich with scents,
Now in the run for newness,
You lost your scents and even your identity too.

Listen, even the hovering butterflies too grumble
They do need to dribble your nectar
Neither the nectar nor the fragrance
Don't you be called as a flower still?"

The flower pop up its eyes wider,
"Oh breeze and butterfly,
What are you grumbling?
Aren't you not with the changes of time?
Now, we are the product of genetic technology:
We do have many varieties and colours,
And feel proud to have modern changes,
Come to our path, change your genes,
Then you can understand us,
Let us move in one rhythm.

Yes, we do change genetically,
Breeze and butterfly mumbled,
And both moved away -
To search for their genes.

Poem 47

True Friend

Things are varying in a world of beauty,
Observations depends on the taste of one,
To distinguish them may seem easily,
Except the living one –man.

Science is in the pioneer of its developments,
Still, true nature of man is unconquerable,
It is a Herculean task to get the result,
Since he can adopt various forms.

We know chameleon who changes its colour,
What for? to abscond from foe's vicinity,
When man smiles like a moon, be careful,
Don't get trapped with the magic spell of it.

There lies a poisonous serpent folded its hood,
Only time can prove the cruel form he attains.
Bitter situations are the criterions of his reality,
That too revealed slowly as he conceals cleverly.

Birds crowd on trees in spring seasons than ever before,
No one in winter except the snow clad leaves,
Friends are more in the zenith of our glory,
Alas, tears only while we are in sorrows.

Better seek friends among dumb creatures,
As they are more reliable than man.

Poem 48

Sons Of Sea

Oh! Sons of sea how brave you are!
Your dawns are blooming in the mid of sea,
The roaring sea or the snow clad sky,
Nothing can besiege you from the toil.

You row and row till arms get tired.
The torn ropes, the age old boats,
Never help you to get a good catch,
At the huts many eyes are waiting,
Without closing the lids slightly.

You are in the long run to search,
A worthwhile pearl which you never get,
You weave bright and colourful dreams.
Which fade and vanish suddenly.
Like the waves wash away the sands on shore.

In the milky moon light you sob and sob,
Thinking of the unending sorrows in life,
No one there to share your sorrows,
Other than the sand and lashing waves.

Your untiring enthusiasm awakes again,
Like phoenix to fight against the odds of life.

Poem 49

Mother

Oh! Mother my sweet heart,
The ecstasy you sprinkle is high,
You embrace me with tender care,
I forget myself in your presence.

You try hard to make both ends meet,
Dedicate yourself for a noble cause,
None can measure the fathom of your love,
Which is more deeper than the oceans.

There are uncles, cousins we get,
But, mother is a reality in every sense.

You are a rare union of bliss and sympathy,
No substitute for your in the world,
Your heart is a unique court,
Forgives surreptitious and horrible sins.

You are the truth an everlasting truth,
Like day and night and sun and stars.

In beauty you are superior,
Than rising stars and sunken sun,
Unheralded heroine of my life,
I bow my head at your feet.

Poem 50

Grazing Feelings

Scribbling letters, shapeless letters,
Like the pyre emits the fumes,
Some notes, rare notes I write, but –
Appear meaningless on the page.

Utter tranquility is brooding on me,
The sky is empty, hardly no clouds.
Stillness shadows and covers all,
Without leaving any gap.

An eye opens on time,
As cruelty leads the streets,
We, helpless, press our fists,
Like a man who catches a hay,
For an escape while drowning.

Carrying season on the hand,
The breeze blows, but relinquish,
No rhythm or ripples in the move,
Resembling mind's silence at night.

Now my mind turns as a dark room,
No colour or brightness,
Do I keep the window open,
For a ray to penetrate here.

A snail may feel more comfort,
Though the shell is a burden,
I can't be a hermit brood in silence,
And wish to free my tongue for a prattle.

Words, words, just fly in the air,
Slipping from mouth to dry:
No where it nests, rolls again,
And mingle with the sobbing at the huts.

Ha! serenity may be more meaningful,
When distress perch like swallows,
Or a hidden fear crawls in the mind,
And surged glitters beyond horizon.

A lonely sun is visible in the sky,
I long for a beam to shine upon me,
All my efforts are vanquished suddenly,
And lost my language in the middle.

My gloom and anxiety are erased,
And a tiny green shot appeared there,
A sudden gleam in the twilight too
So easy, for any imagination to graze.

Now a poem flows in me,
Emotions cannot be still any more,
Words fly and fill everywhere,
With a soothing and scenting effect.

Poem 51

Inequality

Inequality is common and spreads everywhere,
The byproduct of intolerance is inequality,
Inequality in gender, in work and in everything,
The main victims are women and children.

Inequality creeps more in under developed nations,
And gender equality plays major roles,
What a pity! Women are not treated equally,
Not to visit even the worship places of men deities.

In older times, inside the caves,
Were we not together leaning on the wet walls?
Even in hunting, preparing fields for cultivation;
That time we were only man and woman -
Without gender discriminations.

In some culture, status of women too low,
They are treated as a machine for reproduction,
Or as toys to pacify the sexual instinct of men,
Neither they allowed for education nor free thinking.

Is the world revolving backwards?
Superstitions and gender equality cross -
beyond the earth,
Women, the have-nots, are exploited everywhere,
In wages, in status, in life and what not?

Law is there for everything.
But, in most places, it seems like scarecrow,
Law only for the poor and downtrodden:
The rich, the influential are always above laws,
And calmly sleep under the safe zone roofs.

Printed in the United States
By Bookmasters